WRITERS AND THEIR WORK NO. 125

Edward FitzGerald

by JOANNA RICHARDSON

Published for The British Council
and The National Book League
by Longmans, Green & Co.

Two shillings and sixpence net

Edward FitzGerald (1809-1883) is best known to later generations as the translator of the Rubáiyát of Omar Khayyám, which was first published anonymously in 1859. He was also the author of some of the most charming letters ever written in English, which were first published forty years after his famous rendering from the Persian. Miss Joanna Richardson treats of every side of FitzGerald's genius. 'Like all great men of letters', she says, 'he cannot be neatly classified. He belongs to, and stands apart from, his age.'

Miss Richardson has already published studies of Fanny Brawne, Théophile Gautier, Sarah Bernhardt and others. She has in preparation a selection from the Works and Letters of FitzGerald.

Bibliographical Series
of Supplements to 'British Book News'
on Writers and Their Work

★

GENERAL EDITOR
Bonamy Dobrée

¶ EDWARD FITZGERALD was born at Bredfield, Suffolk on 31 March 1809. He died at Merton Rectory, Norfolk, on 14 June 1883.

EDWARD FITZGERALD
from a photograph by CADE OF IPSWICH

EDWARD FITZGERALD

by
JOANNA RICHARDSON

'I think one should only hand over a presentable Likeness of oneself to those who have a Regard for one: and they, as well as I, must *believe* in the Likeness. . . .'—EDWARD FITZGERALD.

PUBLISHED FOR
THE BRITISH COUNCIL
and the NATIONAL BOOK LEAGUE
by LONGMANS, GREEN & CO.

LONGMANS, GREEN & CO. LTD.
6 & 7 Clifford Street, London W.1
Thibault House, Thibault Square, Cape Town
605–611 Lonsdale Street, Melbourne C.1

LONGMANS, GREEN & CO. INC.
119 West 40th Street, New York 18

LONGMANS, GREEN & CO.
20 Cranfield Road, Toronto 16

ORIENT LONGMANS PRIVATE LTD.
Calcutta   Bombay   Madras
Delhi   Hyderabad   Dacca

First published in 1960
© Joanna Richardson 1960

PR
4703
.R5

Printed in Great Britain by Unwin Brothers Limited
Woking and London

CONTENTS

I THE LIFE   *page* 7

II. THE MAN OF LETTERS AND TRANSLATOR 16

III. THE LETTER-WRITER 30

    A SELECT BIBLIOGRAPHY 39

EDWARD FITZGERALD

I. THE LIFE

On 31 March 1809, at Bredfield, some seven miles out of Ipswich, Mary Frances Purcell (*née* Fitz-Gerald) gave birth to her seventh child.
Edward, for so she named him, entered a distinguished family. The FitzGeralds, who traced their descent from the Dukes of Tuscany and Earls of Kildare, were among the most eminent Anglo-Norman families in Ireland. The Purcells had come to England with William the Conqueror. As for Mary Purcell, she was not only well descended, but she was blessed with Junoesque beauty and strong character. We are told that she was 'a very fine woman, but *a bad Mother*'; and certainly she kept at an Olympian distance from her children. Yet Edward's childhood was far from unhappy. He remembered watching from his nursery window as his father and the squire set out in their pink hunting habits; he remembered eating beef and plum pudding and drinking loyal toasts to mark the first anniversary of Waterloo. He remembered vividly how, when he was seven, the family had gone to live in France, and they had seen the royal hunt near Saint-Germain:

> Louis XVIII first, with his *Gardes du Corps*, in blue and silver: then Monsieur (afterwards Charles X) with *his* Guard in green and gold—French horns blowing—'tra, tra, tra' (as Madame de Sévigné says), through the lines of chestnut and limes—in flower. And then *Madame* (of Angoulême) standing up in her carriage, blear-eyed, dressed in white with her waist at her neck—standing up in the carriage at a corner of the wood to curtsey to the English assembled there—my mother among them. This was in 1817 ... I saw, and see it all.

The Purcells lived in Saint-Germain and Paris until, in 1818, Mary's father died, and she became the owner of several handsome estates and, it was said, the wealthiest commoner in England. She and her husband now adopted the name of FitzGerald ('I somehow,' wrote Edward, 'detest my own scrolloping surname') and returned to Bredfield. Edward was promptly sent to the Grammar School at Bury St. Edmunds.

The school was blessed with an enlightened headmaster and an outstanding academic record. Edward proved himself an erratic pupil; but at Bury St. Edmunds he formed his devoted friendships with William Bodham Donne (a descendant of John Donne, the poet); James Spedding, the future editor of Bacon and 'the wisest man I have ever known'; and John Mitchell Kemble, son of Charles Kemble, the actor, and brother of Fanny. His schooldays were unusually happy, and in middle age he could still revisit the town to enjoy 'a Biscuit and a Pint of Sherry' and to gaze affectionately on the old Abbey Gate.

In 1826 he matriculated at Trinity College, Cambridge; and the pattern of Bury St. Edmunds was repeated. Again the curriculum took second place. The honours degree meant keen competition and he chose to read for a pass degree. He read widely, but not, of course, the books prescribed by his tutors; he also formed further intimate friendships: one of them, in his final year, being with Thackeray. Early in 1830 he took a mediocre degree, and embarked upon his apparently aimless life.

It might be more true to say that FitzGerald's allowance of £300 permitted him to follow his fancies, rather than settle down to a calling; and after a brief visit to Paris, he came home to practise his social theories. 'Tell Thackeray,' he wrote to a friend, 'that he is never to invite me to his house, as I intend never to go. . . . I cannot stand seeing new faces in the polite circles. You must know that I am going to become a great bear: and have got all sorts of Utopian ideas into my head about society.'

At twenty-one he adopted his lifelong principle of 'plain living and high thinking'. In 1833 he adopted a diet in which bread and fruit were the staple foods; and his life took on the 'even gray paper character' that it would always retain. Reacting, perhaps, against the luxurious life of his parents, resenting 'the espalier of London dinner-table company', he determined to fling out his branches in his own way. He rented lodgings in Soho or Bloomsbury; and his greatest London pleasures were browsing in bookshops, visiting galleries, and enjoying the company of his bachelor friends. When he was not in London, he would roam about the country, visiting friends and relations and places of interest, keeping, as he said, 'on the windy side of care', and writing letters. 'I suppose it must seem strange to you', he wrote to a Cambridge friend, 'that I should like writing letters . . . However, here I see no companions, so I am pleased to talk to my old friend John Allen: which indeed keeps alive my humanity very much.' 'I have such love of you, and of myself', he added, a few days later, 'that once every week, at least, I feel spurred on by a sort of gathering up of feelings, to vent myself in a letter upon you. . . . I am sorry to say that I have a very young-lady-like partiality to writing to those that I love.'

Among those he loved were William Makepeace Thackeray and Alfred Tennyson; and when he thought of Thackeray, 'the cockles of his heart were warmed':

> The chair that Will sat in, I sit in the best;
> The tobacco is sweetest which Willy hath blest;
> And I never found out that my wine tasted ill
> When a tear would drop in it for thinking of Will . . .

He eagerly followed Thackeray's literary fortunes; he offered to help him in his financial reverses; he wrote him some of his most spirited letters. And even when Thackeray became 'a little spoiled by London praise, and some consequent Egotism', FitzGerald still considered him 'a very fine fellow'. Just before he died, the novelist was asked which, of all his friends, he had cared for most; he is said to have answered: 'Why, dear old Fitz, to be sure.'

As for Tennyson, FitzGerald watched his career with critical interest: 'Tennyson', he once wrote in anger, 'thinks more about his bowels and nerves than about the Laureate wreath he was bound to inherit.... How are we to expect heroic poems from a valetudinary?' But the very criticism indicated affection; and if FitzGerald had small patience with the poet's ills, he still delighted in his company, and generously recognized his distinction:

> Alfred Tennyson [he told Allen, in 1835] staid with me at Ambleside.... I will say no more of Tennyson than that the more I have seen of him, the more cause I have to think him great. His little humours and grumpinesses were so droll, that I was always laughing.... I must however say, further, that I felt what Charles Lamb describes, a sense of depression at times from the overshadowing of a so much more lofty intellect than my own.... Perhaps I have received some benefit in the now more distinct consciousness of my dwarfishness....

The self-effacement and modesty were typical of FitzGerald; and his affection was reciprocated, for the poet wrote: 'I had no truer friend: he was one of the kindliest of men, and I have never known one of so fine and delicate a wit.'

In 1837 FitzGerald took possession of Boulge Cottage; it stood outside the gates of Boulge Hall, the family estate near Bredfield. Here, in this doleful place, with a black retriever, a cat, a housekeeper, Mrs. Faiers, and, in time, a parrot, Beauty Bob, FitzGerald settled down to a serenity which seemed a pirated copy of the peace of God. To his friends such peace must have seemed astonishing, for the walls of the cottage were as thin as a sixpence, the windows refused to shut, and the thatch was 'perforated by lascivious sparrows'. But here, wrote the occupant, 'I sit, read, smoke, and become very wise, and am already quite beyond earthly things'.

And so, in his twenties and thirties, the genteel gipsy lived the set life of middle age: 'A little more folding of the hands—the same faces—the same fields—the same thoughts occurring at the same turns of road—this is all I have to tell of; nothing at all added—but the summer gone.'

It would, however, be wrong to assume that FitzGerald led the life of an indolent recluse. He not only kept in touch with his friends by correspondence and visits, but he read voluminously. He became close friends with the local wits; Bernard Barton, the Quaker poet, and George Crabbe, vicar of Bredfield and the poet's son. In 1840 he attended Carlyle's lectures on 'Heroes and Hero Worship'; and, two years later, he was introduced to the awesome Scottish author. The meeting was fortunate: Carlyle, who was working on Oliver Cromwell, had recently gone to Naseby to identify the Cromwellian battlefield; it so happened that Naseby was part of the large FitzGerald estates, and FitzGerald knew it well. He corrected Carlyle's mistaken conclusions, and set labourers to work to dig at certain spots where (according to tradition) the main action had been fought; and, on the fourth day, a labourer reported that he had discovered bones. 'Clearly enough', cried Carlyle in triumph, 'you are upon the very battle-ground . . . the opening of that burial-heap blazes strangely in my thoughts.' Carlyle's *Cromwell* owed much to FitzGerald; and FitzGerald owed to Naseby his friendship with Carlyle, which lasted till the historian's death thirty-nine years later.

It was a Suffolk friend who was destined to draw FitzGerald towards the writing of his masterpiece. Edward Byles Cowell was an Ipswich merchant by force of circumstance; he was a scholar by inclination. Latin, Greek and French did not satisfy his ardour for languages; he studied Persian, Spanish, Italian, Old Norse and Sanskrit. Although he was hardly nineteen when he met FitzGerald about 1845, he had already established himself as an Oriental scholar with his translations of Persian poetry. In 1847 he married Elizabeth Charlesworth, the daughter of a local clergyman; and FitzGerald, who admired Cowell's intellectual powers, and was deeply attached to his wife, became a frequent visitor at their Suffolk cottage. In this benevolent atmosphere he began 'to nibble at Spanish: at their old Ballads; which are fine things. . . . I have also bounced through a play of Calderón'. By the end of 1852, when the Cowells had moved to Oxford, he had translated one of Calderón's plays; the following summer appeared *Six Dramas of Calderón. Freely Translated by Edward FitzGerald*. One wet Sunday, at Oxford, Cowell 'suggested Persian to him and guaranteed to teach the grammar in a day. The book was Jones's Grammar, the illustrations to which are nearly all from Hafiz. FitzGerald . . . went on to read Hafiz closely'. By October 1853 he was translating Sádi; and for the next eighteen months he studied Persia and Persian poetry. In 1856 he published his version of Jámí's allegory *Salámán and Absál* as a 'little monument' to his Persian studies with Cowell. It was also a monument to departing friends; for Cowell sailed that summer to become professor of English history at the Presidency College, Calcutta.

The departure of his guide and friend, and of the gently inspiring Elizabeth, was not, however, for FitzGerald, the calamity of the year. Early in November, inspired by a wildly mistaken sense of chivalry, he married the plain, middle-aged and strictly conventional daughter of Bernard Barton. There could hardly have been a more ill-assorted couple; and in August 1857 they separated, and 'if', wrote FitzGerald, 'people want to go further for the cause of all this Blunder than the fact of two People of very determined habits and Temper, first trying to change them at close on fifty—they may lay nine-tenths of the Blame on me'.

★ ★ ★

Just before the Cowells left for India in July 1856, FitzGerald and his friend had 'read some curious Infidel and Epicurean Tetrastichs by a Persian of the Eleventh Century—as Savage against Destiny etc. as Manfred—but mostly of Epicurean Pathos of this kind—"Drink—for the Moon will often come round to look for us in this Garden and find us not"'. These infidel verses were the *Rubáiyát*, or quatrains, of Omar Khayyám, which Cowell had discovered in a Persian manuscript in the Bodleian Library at Oxford. He had copied the verses for FitzGerald; and, in the spring of 1857, in the midst of his disastrous marriage, FitzGerald had found that Omar 'breathes a sort of Consolation!' About the middle of June he received a copy of a second Omar manuscript, which Cowell had discovered in Calcutta; and on 14 July 1857, the anniversary of his parting from his friend, as he was walking in his rose-filled Norfolk garden, a translation of a stanza formed in FitzGerald's mind:

> I long for wine! oh Saki of my Soul,
> Prepare thy Song and fill the morning Bowl;
> For this first Summer month that brings the Rose
> Takes many a Sultán with it as it goes.

Within the next six months he had translated many of the *Rubáiyát*. He had become (as he signed himself) Edward FitzOmar. 'In truth', he wrote to Cowell, 'I take old Omar rather more as my property than yours: he and I are more akin, are we not? You see all [his] Beauty, but you don't feel with him in some respects as I do. . . .' He sent thirty-five of his 'less wicked' stanzas to *Fraser's Magazine*, warning the editor that the verse might be 'rather dangerous among his divines'. The editor apparently agreed; and by November 1858 even the patient FitzGerald was moved to action. He retrieved his manuscript, added forty quatrains, and had two hundred and fifty copies printed and bound in brown paper. He kept forty, and handed the rest to Quaritch, a London bookseller, who specialized in Oriental works. On 9 April 1859, the *Rubáiyát* was advertised as 'just published', and review copies were sent to various magazines. FitzGerald's name was not on the title-page.

* * *

While FitzGerald was absorbed in translating and publishing Omar, the course of his private life had been changing. The death of friends had broken some of his last ties with early manhood, his final ties with inland Suffolk, and he had begun to turn seawards for happiness:

> My chief amusement in Life [he told Cowell] is Boating, on River and Sea. The Country about here is the Cemetery of so many of my oldest Friends: and the petty race of Squires who have succeeded only use the Earth for an *Investment*: cut down every old Tree: level every Violet Bank: and make the old Country of my Youth hideous to me in my Decline. There are fewer Birds to be heard, as fewer Trees for them to resort to. So I get to the Water: where Friends are not buried nor Pathways stopt up. . . .

He haunted Lowestoft, on the Suffolk coast, where, in season, the herring boats unloaded their teeming catches. The sea always kept alive, and the streets of Lowestoft were full of rugged sailors, 'the old English stuff', 'obstinate Fellows with wonderful Shoulders', 'a very fine Race of Men, far superior to those in Regent Street'. FitzGerald's admiration of physical vigour, of 'Sea Language', as he called it, drew him to the tavern kitchens at Aldeburgh, to smoke, drink grog, and sing with the sailors. The small craft he sailed on the River Deben was replaced by a new boat, specially built, with a crew of two. At last, in 1863, he ordered a 43-foot schooner: the *Scandal*, which was his summer home for eight years:

> You must think I have become very nautical, by all this [he confessed]: haul away at ropes, swear, dance Hornpipes, etc. But it is not so: I simply sit in my Boat or Vessel as in a moving Chair, dispensing a little Grog and Shag to those who do the work.

This idyllic existence had, alas, to be changed in winter for the monotonous life of his lodgings in Woodbridge, 'all the faded tapestry of country town life'. Here, in inland Suffolk, he whiled away the weeks by reading, translating, and writing letters. In the spring of 1864, however, he bought a cottage on the northern outskirts of the town; he enlarged it, engaged a couple as caretakers, and furnished it as a summer house for friends and relations; it was characteristic of him that for seven years he himself persisted in staying in Woodbridge and not becoming the laird of Little Grange.

* * *

In 1874 FitzGerald finally took possession of what he called his *château*: Little Grange, where he was to spend the remainder of his life. But a sadness settled over him, and to his friend Aldis Wright he expressed the wish that the sword would fall:

> If I do not write [this on 12 June 1883], it is because I have absolutely nothing to tell you that you have not known for the last twenty years. Here I live still, reading, and being read to, part of my time; walking abroad three or four times a day, or night, in spite of wakening a Bronchitis, which has lodged like the household 'Brownie' within; pottering about my Garden (as I have just been doing) and snipping off dead Roses like Miss Tox; and now and then a visit to the neighbouring Seaside, and a splash to Sea in one of the Boats. I never see a new Picture, nor hear a note of Music except when I drum out some old Tune in Winter on an Organ, which might almost be carried about the Streets with a handle to turn, and a Monkey on the top of it. So I go on, living a life far too comfortable as compared with that of better, and wiser men: but ever expecting a reverse in health such as my seventy-five years are subject to. . . .
> Tomorrow I am going (for my one annual Visit) to G. Crabbe's. . . .

In all probability this was FitzGerald's last letter. Next day, 13 June, he left for his annual visit to Merton Rectory. On 14 June, Crabbe entered his room to find him 'as if sleeping peacefully but quite dead'.

Five days later, FitzGerald was buried at Boulge. At his feet, in time, they planted a Persian rose-tree grown from the tree by the grave of Omar Khayyám.

II. THE MAN OF LETTERS AND TRANSLATOR

FitzGerald's first published book appeared in 1849: his edition of the *Poems and Letters of Bernard Barton*. His 'editorial mind' had reduced the nine volumes of Barton's works to some 200 pages. It was a monument to what FitzGerald called his 'Irish accuracy'. 'Some of the poems I take entire,' he told Donne, 'some half—some only a few stanzas, and these dovetailed together—with a change of word, or even of a line here and there, to give them logic and fluency . . . I am sure I have distilled many pretty little poems out of long dull ones which the world has discarded.' This free adaptation was characteristic of FitzGerald's methods of work, and it would purse a good many academic brows; but he prefaced the book with a memoir of his Quaker friend which was lucid, candid and charming.

In 1851 (again without his name) he published a more important work: *Euphranor, A Dialogue on Youth*. On one of his visits to Cambridge, FitzGerald had been shocked by 'the hard-reading, pale, dwindled students walking along the Observatory road'. *Euphranor* is written as a Platonic dialogue between himself, in the character of a Cambridge doctor, Euphranor, a bookish graduate, and three students: one hard-working, one idle, and one the admirable *uomo universale*. It is a criticism of contemporary English education. FitzGerald charges the schools with neglect of the physical exercise and practical training which will fit a man 'for the campaign of ordinary Life. . . . At any rate', fit him 'not only to shoot the Pheasant and hunt the Fox, but even to sit on the Bench of Magistrates—or even of Parliament—not unprovided with a quotation or two from Horace or Virgil'. FitzGerald 'had it at heart the Book should be read', and posterity can appreciate its progressive thought and wisdom. *Euphranor* is, for the most part, rather heavy and stilted, but the final description of the May Races at Cambridge won the admiration of Tennyson; it is a fine and musical passage of prose:

We walk'd along the fields by the Church ... cross'd the Ferry, and mingled with the crowd upon the opposite shore; Townsmen and Gownsmen, with the tassel'd Fellow-commoner sprinkled here and there—Reading men and Sporting men—Fellows, and even Masters of College, not indifferent to the prowess of their respective Crews—all these, conversing on all sorts of topics, from the slang in Bell's *Life* to the last new German Revelation, and moving in everchanging groups down the shore of the river, at whose farther bend was a little knot of Ladies gathered upon a green knoll faced and illuminated by the beams of the setting sun. Beyond which point was at length heard some indistinct shouting, which gradually increased, until 'They are off—they are coming!' suspended other conversation among ourselves; and suddenly the head of the first boat turn'd the corner; and then another close upon it; and then a third; the crews pulling with all their might compacted into perfect rhythm; and the crowd on shore turning round to follow along with them waving hats and caps, and cheering, 'Bravo, St. John's!' 'Go it, Trinity!'—the high crest and blowing forelock of Phidippus's mare, and he himself shouting encouragement to his crew, conspicuous over all, until the boats reaching us, we also were caught up in the returning tide of spectators, and hurried back toward the goal; where we arrived just in time to see the Ensign of Trinity lowered from its pride of place, and the Eagle of St. John's soaring there instead. Then, waiting a little while to hear how the winner had won, and the loser lost, and watching Phidippus engaged in eager conversation with his defeated brethren, I took Euphranor and Lexilogus under either arm, (Lycion having got into better company elsewhere) and walk'd home with them across the meadow leading to the town, whither the dusky troops of Gownsmen with all their confused voices seem'd as it were evaporating in the twilight, while a Nightingale began to be heard among the flowering Chestnuts of Jesus.

FitzGerald's next work: *Polonius: A Collection of Wise Saws and Modern Instances* (1852), was an anthology of quotations on such topics as honesty, riches and liberty, vanity and charity. He predicted that it would be a losing affair, and the sale was certainly limited.

The following year appeared *Six Dramas of Calderón*.

Freely Translated by Edward FitzGerald. The selection was designed to 'give a fair idea of Calderón's Spanish Life'; and the translator, with his usual Irish freedom, 'while faithfully trying to retain what was fine and efficient; sunk, reduced, altered, and replaced, much that seemed not'. The result was a series of plays which savoured little of the dictionary: vigour, comedy and character, all are evident; and the moments of lyrical and dramatic poetry are not wanting. One recalls the words of Manuel to Pedro in *Gil Perez, the Gallician*:

> I must to sea, joining the armament
> That sails to plant the banner of the church
> Over the golden turrets of the north...

It is a felicitous piece of blank verse. Or, again, one recalls the conversation of Serafina and Alvaro in *The Painter of His Own Dishonour*; it shows a quite remarkable ease of manner:

Serafina ... My husband's love for me, and mine for him,
My station and my name, all have so changed me,
That winds and waves might sooner overturn
Not the oak only,
But the eternal rock on which it grows,
Than you my heart, though sea and sky themselves
Join'd in the tempest of your sighs and tears.

Alvaro But what if I remember other times
When Serafina was no stubborn oak,
Resisting wind and wave, but a fair flower
That open'd to the sun of early love,
And follow'd him along the golden day:
No barren heartless rock,
But a fair temple in whose sanctuary
Love was the idol, daily and nightly fed
With sacrifice of one whole human heart...

> Serafina,
> Why talk to me of ages, when the account
> Of my misfortune and your cruelty
> Measures itself by hours, and not by years!
> It was but yesterday you loved me, yes,
> Loved me, and (let the metaphor run on)
> I never will believe it ever was,
> Or is, or ever can be possible
> That the fair flower so soon forgot the sun
> To which so long she owed and turn'd her beauty,
> To love the baser mould in which she grew:
> Or that the temple could so soon renounce
> Her old god, true god too while he was there,
> For any cold and sober deity
> Which you may venerate, but cannot love . . .

Only the academic would quibble here about linguistic niceties; but, alas! if FitzGerald's friends allowed him his liberty of translation, the critics were less indulgent.

In 1856, undeterred, he published a free version of Jámí's allegory, *Salámán and Absál*. 'It shows', wrote a critic, 'some poetic feeling, a diligent use of the dictionary, but a very moderate acquaintance with Persian . . . mistakes are numerous. . . . As a first attempt, however, to make Jámí accessible to the English reader, this little volume is deserving of commendation.' FitzGerald's next book was to be a classic.

* * *

We have seen how, in the summer of 1856, he had discovered the quatrains of Omar Khayyám, and had found them a 'kind of Consolation' for his disastrous marriage and profound depression. In the spring of 1857 he had written to Garcin de Tassy, a French scholar of Persian literature, asking if there were any Omar manuscripts in Paris. In May he confessed to Cowell: 'I think I shall become a bore . . . by all this Translation: but it amuses me without any labour, and I really think I have the faculty of making some things readable which others have hitherto left unreadable.' In June he had 'put away almost all Books, except Omar Khayyám: which I could not help looking over in a Paddock covered with Buttercups and brushed by a delicious Breeze'. He turned some of the quatrains into Latin. That month he received a copy of a second Omar manuscript, which Cowell had discovered in Calcutta, and decided 'poor old Omar . . . is the best Persian I have seen'. 'June over!' he added in July. 'A thing I think of with Omar-like sorrow. And the Roses here are blowing—and going—as abundantly as even in Persia. I am still at Geldestone, and still looking at Omar. . . .' He was, in fact, increasingly fascinated by the poem, and by the poet himself, who seemed to anticipate his own sorrows, doubts and vexations, his own affection for Epicurean ease. In July, a translated stanza crystallized in his mind, and within the next six months he had turned many more into English. The first version of the *Rubáiyát* seems to have filled his mind and heart, and to have grown by a slow, generic growth. It grew, like an original poem, with his own mood and experience.

Translation is, however, hardly the word to apply to FitzGerald's *Rubáiyát*, 'very unliteral as it is. Many Quatrains,' he confessed, 'are mashed together: and something lost, I doubt, of Omar's Simplicity which is so much a Virtue in him. But there it is, such as it is.' 'I suppose,' he added, 'very few People have ever taken such Pains in Translation as I have: though certainly not to be literal. But at all Cost, a Thing must live: with a transfusion of one's own worse Life if one can't retain the Original's better. Better a live Sparrow than a stuffed Eagle.'

It is in this spirit that the *Rubáiyát* of FitzGerald must be judged. It is less a translation than a feat of marvellous poetic transfusion. We shall not find a precise English version of the original, following the Persian line by line. We shall find instead a fusion of the Oxford and Calcutta manuscripts, sometimes shortened, sometimes lengthened, often changed in sequence, and inspired by the strangely sympathetic genius of an English writer who was born some seven centuries after Omar died.

* * *

Few remarkable poems in English literature have been published so unobtrusively, or enjoyed a greater romance. FitzGerald himself gave away a mere three copies; and 'I hardly know,' he wrote to Cowell, 'why I print any of these things, which nobody buys; and I scarce now see the few I give them to. But when one has done one's best, and is sure that that best is better than so many will take pains to do, though far from the best that *might be done*, one likes to make an end of the matter by Print.' Cowell, a pious man, was shocked at the *Rubáiyát*; the reviewers ignored it. The sales, if any, were almost negligible, and for nearly two years the five-shilling pamphlets lay on Quaritch's shelves. Then, in 1861, they were reduced to 1d. and dumped into the bargain box outside his shop; and there they stayed until the editor of the *Saturday Review* happened to browse over a copy, and bought a number of them for his friends.

The *Rubáiyát* had entered the literary world; Rossetti told Swinburne of the discovery and both bought copies. 'Next day,' recorded Swinburne, 'when we returned for more, the price was raised, to the iniquitous and exorbitant sum of twopence. . . . But we were extravagant enough to invest in a few more copies, even at that scandalous price.' The Pre-Raphaelites were aglow with enthusiasm. Swinburne soon after took the rhyme scheme and almost the same metre for *Laus Veneris*; he also presented the *Rubáiyát* to Burne-Jones, who copied it for many of his friends. When Burne-Jones showed the poem to Ruskin in 1863, the critic wrote a note 'To the Translator of Omar Khayyám'; Burne-Jones was told to deliver it when the anonymous poet was discovered:

My dear and very dear Sir

I do not know in the least who you are, but I do with all my soul pray you to find and translate some more of Omar Khayyám for us: I never did—till this day—read anything so glorious, to my mind, as this poem. . . .

In 1868 FitzGerald published a longer edition of the *Rubáiyát*. He remained anonymous; and when, in 1872, the third edition appeared, he was still 'the great Un-nameable'. But, by a strange series of chances, Burne-Jones had shown the *Rubáiyát* to a visiting American critic, Charles Eliot Norton; and in October 1869 Norton acclaimed the poem in the *North American Review*. The article created a 'little Craze' in the United States; the third and fourth editions of the *Rubáiyát* were printed, and Fanny Kemble's daughter, who knew FitzGerald's other translations, wrote to ask him if he was the author. In her limited Philadelphian circle the mystery was solved.

In 1876 FitzGerald was formally acknowledged as the translator of the *Rubáiyát*, but, alas, not until he had died did 'the little Craze' for the poem grow like the mustard-seed across the world. His *Rubáiyát* has been set to music. It has been parodied. There are now at least one hundred and eighty editions, and translations into Gaelic, German, French, Swedish, Spanish, Sanskrit, Italian, Afrikaans and Yiddish.

* * *

It was said by the enemies of Omar Khayyám that his study of astronomy had only prompted him to disbelief. In fact he was neither an atheist nor an agnostic. He was an honest scholar, a student of Lucretius, who rebelled against the bigotry and dogma of Mohammedanism. He satirized those who substituted ritual for worship. And, much concerned with the problem of evil, he challenged the benevolence of a God Who ordained both good and evil and yet punished man for sin. He was bewildered by the riddle of life, and he consoled himself (as even the Victorians consoled themselves) with the delights of physical existence.

FitzGerald shared Omar Khayyám's contempt for sanctimony, bigotry and hypocrisy. A widely-read Victorian, he observed the opening skirmishes of the long struggle between modern science and religion (his *Rubáiyát* appeared in the same year as *The Origin of Species*). He was more outspoken than his contemporaries; but he was no more unorthodox than many who confessed their doubts while they sought for faith. Voltaire, the true intellectual eighteenth-century sceptic, had declared that if God did not exist, mankind would have to invent Him. Leconte de Lisle, FitzGerald's contemporary, was a bitter atheist. FitzGerald himself, an Anglican and a frequent churchgoer, never expressed any doubt of the existence of God: he was only sceptical of Old Testament theology (how, in Darwin's day, could he believe in Adam and Eve?) and the life after death. In the eleventh-century *Rubáiyát* he discovered an anticipation of nineteenth-century thought: 'a desperate sort of Thing, unfortunately found at the bottom of all thinking Men's minds; but made Music of'. This natural sympathy drew him to Omar Khayyám, and drew the Victorians and posterity after him. The *Rubáiyát* expressed, in poetry, the doubts, fears, aspirations and regrets of the great mass of mankind. 'It is the only one of all my Great Works that ever has been asked for', FitzGerald wrote when the second edition appeared. 'I am persuaded, *because* of the Wickedness, which is now at the heart of so much Goodness! Not that the Persian has anything at all new: but he has dared to say it, as Lucretius did: and now it is put into tolerable English music—That is all.'

In his *Rubáiyát*, which were epigrams struck off at intervals during his life, Omar Khayyám had attempted no consistency of belief, no continuity of thought. It was FitzGerald who grouped the quatrains already allied in thought, and imposed consistency, indeed dramatic unity upon them. His second and longer version, he explained, 'gave Omar's thoughts room to turn in, as also the Day which the poem occupied. He begins with Dawn pretty sober and contemplative: then as he thinks and drinks, grows savage, blasphemous, &c., and then again sobers down into melancholy at nightfall'.

FitzGerald's poem opens with the dawn, and with the invocation that Horace, Ronsard and Herrick before him had sung. *Carpe diem* . . . *Eheu fugaces.* . . .

> Dreaming when Dawn's Left Hand was in the Sky,
> I heard a Voice within the Tavern cry,
> 'Awake, my Little ones, and fill the Cup
> Before Life's Liquor in its Cup be dry.' . . .
>
> Come, fill the Cup, and in the Fire of Spring
> The Winter Garment of Repentance fling:
> The Bird of Time has but a little way
> To fly—and Lo! the Bird is on the Wing.

The poet urges us to enjoy material pleasures: the bread, the wine, the poetry, the lover, and not to dismiss the present joy for the mere prospect of paradise. We must, like the rose, spend our treasure in a day; we must remember that even the rich and the mighty must come to dust, and that we shall follow them:

> Ah, my Belovéd, fill the cup that clears
> TO-DAY of past Regrets and future Fears—
> To-morrow?—Why, To-morrow I may be
> Myself with Yesterday's Sev'n Thousand Years . . .
>
> Ah, make the most of what we yet may spend,
> Before we too into the Dust descend;
> Dust into Dust, and under Dust, to lie,
> Sans Wine, sans Song, sans Singer, and—sans End!

The sages of the world, for all their wisdom, are turned to dust; and the sum of all their knowledge is uncertainty:

> There was a Door to which I found no Key:
> There was a Veil past which I could not see:
>   Some little Talk awhile of ME and THEE
> There seem'd—and then no more of THEE and ME.
>
> Then to the rolling Heav'n itself I cried,
> Asking, 'What Lamp had Destiny to guide
>   Her little Children stumbling in the Dark?'
> And—'A blind Understanding!' Heav'n replied.

As the day lengthens and the poet broods, he is moved to anger by the injustice of predestination and the cruel indifference of God:

> Into this Universe, and *why* not knowing,
> Nor *whence*, like Water willy-nilly flowing:
>   And out of it, as Wind along the Waste,
> I know not *whither*, willy-nilly blowing.
>
> What, without asking, hither hurried *whence?*
> And, without asking, *whither* hurried hence?
>   Another and another Cup to drown
> The Memory of this Impertinence!

Heaven has sent her children into darkness, with only their blind understanding to guide them; and they can only find an earthly consolation for their misery, a temporal solution to their spiritual and eternal problems. Men are merely pawns in the chess-game of destiny, and God in Heaven watches the game, uncaring:

> The Ball no Question makes of Ayes and Noes,
> But Right or Left as strikes the Player goes;
>   And He that toss'd Thee down into the Field,
> *He* knows about it all—He knows—HE knows!

Will God, Who set the snares on earth, allow man to be enmeshed, and then impute his fall to transgression? As the poet, with growing fury, reflects on such injustice, he is moved to blasphemy:

> Oh, Thou, who Man of baser Earth did make,
> And who with Eden didst devise the Snake;
> For all the Sin wherewith the Face of Man
> Is blacken'd, Man's Forgiveness give—and take!

And then, as evening draws on, and the wine is finished, and indignation gives way to sober reflection, the poet returns, at last, to lament the passing of youth and the inevitability of death:

> Alas! that Spring should vanish with the Rose!
> That Youth's sweet-scented Manuscript should close!
> The Nightingale that in the Branches sang,
> Ah, whence, and whither flown again, who knows?

> Ah Love! could thou and I with Fate conspire
> To grasp this sorry Scheme of Things entire,
> Would we not shatter it to bits—and then
> Re-mould it nearer to the Heart's Desire!

The *Rubáiyát*, with its doubts of religion, shocked and fascinated an age of religious upheaval. Its themes remain our constant preoccupations. But, as FitzGerald recognized, it has been the music that has sung the *Rubáiyát* into English literature. We may talk of alliteration, metaphor and scansion, but such analyses do not explain why so many English people find, suddenly, that they know so much of the poem by heart. Whatever the merits of the original, FitzGerald's *Rubáiyát* is a great English poem; and, as he once wrote, 'only God, who made the Rose smell so, knows why such Poems come from the Heart and go to it'.

★ ★ ★

None the less, if one compares a literal translation with

FitzGerald's version one may appreciate a little of his achievement:

> Since no one will be answerable for to-morrow,
> Make happy now this distraught heart.
> Drink wine by the light of the moon, for the moon
> Will seek much, and not find us.

So goes the exact translation of the Oxford manuscript; and FitzGerald recalls it in his two final stanzas:

> Ah, Moon of my Delight who know'st no wane,
> The Moon of Heav'n is rising once again:
> How oft hereafter rising shall she look
> Through this same Garden after me—in vain!
>
> And when Thyself with shining Foot shall pass
> Among the Guests Star-scatter'd on the Grass,
> And in thy joyous Errand reach the Spot
> Where I made one—turn down an empty Glass!

'As poor Omar is one I have great fellow feeling with, I would rather vamp him up again with a few Alterations & Additions than anything else.' So he wrote to his publisher in 1867. He did indeed alter and add to 'poor Omar'. The first edition had 75 stanzas, the second (for which he referred to a French text of Omar as well) 110, the third and fourth 101. Nine stanzas appeared in the second edition only; and the sequence was so radically changed from edition to edition that stanza 44 in the first edition became stanza 73 in the second version and stanza 68 in the third and fourth. Moreover, the stanzas themselves were constantly reformed: the opening stanza was twice altered, and not, one would think, for the better:

> Awake! for Morning in the Bowl of Night
> Has flung the Stone that puts the Stars to Flight:
> And Lo! the Hunter of the East has caught
> The Sultán's Turret in a Noose of Light.

So ran the opening lines in the first edition; in the second version they went:

> Wake! For the Sun beyond yon Eastern height
> Has chased the Session of the Stars from Night;
> And, to the field of Heav'n ascending, strikes
> The Sultán's Turret with a Shaft of Light.

In the third and fourth versions the stanza differed yet again:

> Wake! For the Sun who scatter'd into flight
> The Stars before him from the Field of Night,
> Drives Night along with them from Heav'n, and strikes
> The Sultán's Turret with a Shaft of Light.

These alterations do not always intensify the poetry; and, as FitzGerald pointed out, they do not always make the poem more accurate. 'I daresay Ed^n 1 is better in some respects than 2,' wrote FitzGerald blandly to Quaritch, 'but I think not altogether. . . . I dare say Ed^n 1 best pleased those who read it first: as first Impressions are apt to be strongest. . . . As to the relative fidelity of the two Versions, there isn't a Pin to choose—not in the opening Stanzas you send.'

* * *

After the appearance of the *Rubáiyát*, FitzGerald did not appear publicly in print until Quaritch issued the second edition in 1868. He was not, however, idle during these nine years: his first undertaking after the *Rubáiyát* was to finish his translation of Attár's *Mantik-ut-Tair*, or *Parliament of Birds*. This was published only after his death, but it may be considered here as one of his most inspired translations. The poem is a kind of ornithological *Pilgrim's Progress*. The birds set out on a pilgrimage to the sacred mountain, Káf, in search of Symurgh, a bird of great wisdom; they pass through seven valleys of probation, and many die by the wayside, before the thirty faithful survivors stand, at last, before the Throne, and the Voice addresses them:

> 'Come you lost Atoms to your Centre draw,
> And *be* the Eternal Mirror that you saw:
> Rays that have wander'd into Darkness wide
> Return, and back into your Sun subside.'

Some of FitzGerald's richest poetry may be found in the *Parliament of Birds*. The characters of the birds themselves are brilliantly distinguished:

> Then came the subtle *Parrot* in a coat
> Greener than Greensward, and about his Throat
> A Collar ran of sub-sulphureous Gold;
> And in his Beak a Sugar-plum he troll'd,
> That all his Words with luscious Lisping ran . . .
>
> Then from a Pond, where all day long he kept,
> Waddled the dapper *Duck* demure, adept
> At infinite Ablution, and precise
> In keeping of his Raiment clean and nice.
> And 'Sure of all the Race of Birds', said He,
> 'None for Religious Purity like Me . . .'

As for the philosophy of the poem, it is the very opposite of the *Rubáiyát*. Omar had doubted the benevolence of God; but the *Parliament of Birds*, in a magnificent passage, affirms the divine well-wishing:

> For like a Child sent with a fluttering Light
> To feel his way along a gusty Night
> Man walks the World: again and yet again
> The Lamp shall be by Fits of Passion slain:
> But shall not He who sent him from the Door
> Relight the Lamp once more, and yet once more?

When he had finished the *Parliament of Birds*, FitzGerald, finding that the earlier ones were liked, translated two more plays by Calderón, including the great *La Vida es sueño*, of which his *Such Stuff as Dreams are Made On* is a radical reconstruction. He collected material for a vocabulary of provincial English, and printed glossaries of Suffolk *Sea Words and Phrases*. In 1876 he published 'an impudent Version of the Agamemnon', which was acclaimed as being 'profoundly penetrated with the Æschylean spirit'. In 1880 and 1881 his translations of Sophocles were privately distributed, and in 1882 Quaritch published his *Readings in Crabbe*. During his last years FitzGerald was working on selections from Dryden's *Prefaces*, and a dictionary for 'my dear Sévigné's' correspondence. This last was completed for him after his death by his niece, Mary Kerrich. His projected biography of Charles Lamb never went further than a brief chronology of the essayist's life.

III. THE LETTER-WRITER

FitzGerald has a double claim to immortality. The translator of Omar Khayyám has, perhaps, received his due; the letter-writer remains to be discovered. There is no definitive edition of FitzGerald's correspondence, and this omission is strange and unjust, for he holds so high a place among the English letter-writers that at times he is reminiscent of Keats. One cannot, it is true, trace the same god-like growth of soul and intellect; and yet one can understand why, to FitzGerald, 'poor Keats' little finger' was 'worth all the body' of Shelley. He found, in Keats, his own best genius magnified. FitzGerald's letters, like the letters of Keats, reveal the living, sensual man, with his griefs and humours and pleasures, the lover of life and nature and literature, the possessor of a sharp and loving visual sense, and sometimes they recall the poet by a sudden turn of phrase, by sheer verbal felicity.

FitzGerald's letter-writing was largely dictated by his Irish vitality and his constant solitude. Letters, to him, replaced companionship; they were substitutes for conversation:

> I suppose [he wrote to John Allen in 1834] that people who are engaged in serious ways of life, and are of well filled minds, don't think much about the interchange of letters with any anxiety; but I am an idle fellow, of a very ladylike turn of sentiment: and my friendships are more like loves, I think. Your letter found me reading the Merry Wives of Windsor too: I had been laughing aloud to myself: think of what another coat of happiness came over my former good mood. You are a dear good fellow, and I love you with all my heart and soul.

His zest for life, his warmth of feeling, shone through his correspondence:

> Ah! I wish you were here to talk with me [this again to Allen] now that the warm weather is come at last. Things have been delayed but to be more welcome, and to burst forth twice as thick and beautiful. This is boasting, however, and counting of the chickens before they are hatched: the East winds may again plunge us back into winter: but the sunshine of this morning fills one's pores with jollity, as if one had taken laughing gas....

Country sunshine, flowers and books, gentle domestic ease: these were the elements of FitzGerald's English paradise; and he caught them, as if in amber, in his letters. Irish by birth, he was English at heart. 'Well, say as you will,' he wrote to a friend in Italy, 'there is not, and never was, such a country as Old England.... I am sure no travel would carry me to any land so beautiful, as the good sense, justice and liberality of my good countrymen make this....' A paragraph of FitzGerald, at his best, can bring a whole English landscape into view, and, brilliantly, imply the foreground figure:

> Here is a glorious sunshiny day: all the morning I read about Nero in Tacitus lying at full length on a bench in the garden: a nightingale singing, and some red anemones eyeing the sun

manfully not far off. A funny mixture all this: Nero and the
delicacy of Spring: all very human however. Then at half-past
one lunch on Cambridge cream cheese: then a ride over hill and
dale; then spudding up some weeds from the grass: and then
coming in, I sit down to write to you, my sister winding red
worsted from the back of a chair, and the most delightful little
girl in the world chattering incessantly. So runs the world away.
You think I live in Epicurean ease: but this happens to be a jolly
day: one isn't always well, or tolerably good, the weather is not
always clear, nor nightingales singing, nor Tacitus full of pleasant
atrocity. But such as life is, I believe I have got hold of a good end
of it. . . .

The English countryside (the 'poor mistaken lilac buds',
the 'old Robin ruffled up to his thickest') inspired some
enchanting description; FitzGerald was never entirely happy
away from East Anglia, from the Norfolk and Suffolk
landscapes he knew so well: 'I get radishes to eat for breakfast of a morning,' so he wrote from London in 1844: 'with
them comes a savour of earth that brings all the delicious
gardens of the world back into one's soul, and almost draws
tears from one's eyes.' London disturbed his usual tranquillity; in a brilliant, spontaneous letter to Bernard Barton,
written that same April day, he expressed his nostalgia for
the country, and conjured up a mirage of his ramshackle
cottage:

> When I get back to Boulge, I shall recover my quietude which
> is now all in a ripple. But it is a shame to talk of such things. . . .
> A cloud comes over Charlotte Street and seems as if it were
> sailing softly on the April wind to fall in a blessed shower upon
> the lilac buds and thirsty anemones somewhere in Essex; or, who
> knows?, perhaps at Boulge. Out will run Mrs. Faiers, and with
> red arms and face of woe haul in the struggling windows of the
> cottage, and make all tight. Beauty Bob [the parrot] will cast a
> bird's eye out at the shower, and bless the useful wet. Mr. Loder
> will observe to the farmer for whom he is doing up a dozen of
> Queen's Heads, that it will be of great use: and the farmer will
> agree that his young barleys wanted it much. The German Ocean

will dimple with innumerable pin points, and porpoises rolling near the surface sneeze with unusual pellets of fresh water. . . . Oh this wonderful, wonderful world, and we who stand in the middle of it are all in a maze. . . .

He returned to his cottage to greet the early summer, and sent a fresh pastoral vignette to Frederic Tennyson, the poet's brother and himself a poet:

> I read of mornings; the same old books over and over again, having no command of new ones: walk with my great black dog of an afternoon, and at evening sit with open windows, up to which China roses climb, with my pipe, while the blackbirds and thrushes begin to rustle bedwards in the garden, and the nightingale to have the neighbourhood to herself. We have had such a spring (bating the last ten days) as would have satisfied even you with warmth. And such verdure! white clouds moving over the new fledged tops of oak trees, and acres of grass striving with buttercups. How old to tell of, how new to see!

FitzGerald's love of nature never deserted him: thirty-five years later we find him lamenting the lateness of the spring to Mrs. Kemble:

> Scarce a tinge of Green on the hedgerows; scarce a Bird singing (only once the Nightingale, with a broken Voice), and no flowers in the Garden but the brave old Daffydowndilly, and Hyacinth—which I scarce knew were so hardy. I am quite pleased to find how comfortably they do in my Garden, and look so Chinese gay. Two of my dear Blackbirds have I found dead—of Cold and Hunger, I suppose; but one is even now singing—across that Funeral Bell. This is so, as I write, and tell you—Well: we have Sunshine at last. . . .

FitzGerald's criticism of art, as one might expect, was keen, affectionate, and at times poetic. It is true that his judgement has not always been endorsed: 'I got a look at the National Gallery', so he declared in 1862, 'but the Devotion of one whole Room to Turner seems to me to be a national

Absurdity.' Yet if FitzGerald strangely failed to appreciate Turner, he could pass stringent judgement on the largely representational art of his time; and he could not, for example, persuade himself 'that Frith's veracious Portraitures of people eating Luncheons at Epsom are to be put in the Scale with Raffaelle's impossible Idealisation of the Human made Divine'.

FitzGerald prided himself on collecting pictures: he was fascinated by auction-rooms and dealers' shops, and haunted by pictures that he wished to buy. He enjoyed varnishing and cleaning his collection (and, it must be confessed, even cutting down a canvas on occasion). In 1841 he acquired what he thought was a masterpiece, and dashed off his jubilation to Frederic Tennyson:

> I have just concluded, with all the throes of imprudent pleasure, the purchase of a large picture by Constable, of which, if I can continue in the mood, I will enclose you a sketch. It is very good: but how you and Morton would abuse it! Yet this, being a sketch, escapes some of Constable's faults, and might escape some of your censures. The trees are not splashed with that white sky-mud, which (according to Constable's theory) the Earth scatters up with her wheels in travelling so briskly round the sun; and there is a dash and felicity in the execution that gives one a thrill of good digestion in one's room, and the thought of which makes one inclined to jump over the children's heads in the streets. But if you could see my great enormous Venetian Picture you would be astonished. Does the thought ever strike you, when looking at pictures in a house, that you are to run and jump at one, and go right through it to the other side, as Harlequins do? A steady portrait especially invites one to do so: the quietude of it ironically tempts one to outrage it: one feels it would close again over the panel, like water, as if nothing had happened. . . .

FitzGerald's affection for music, like his affection for art, is reflected in his letters. It is, perhaps, an amateur's affection, an artist's affection, for he expresses it in strongly visual terms. It was, however, for literature, and literature of the most diverse kinds, that he felt the most intense enthusiasm.

'I don't find myself growing old about Poetry', he wrote when he was forty. 'On the contrary.' And again: 'I believe I love poetry almost as much as ever: but then . . . I have not put away childish things, though a man. . . .'

There was nothing childish in his love of poetry, unless it was its very eagerness. He read it, always, with the ardour that breeds true appreciation: he felt it with his heart before his head. He had his natural inclinations: 'I have rather a wish', he wrote, 'to tie old Wordsworth's volume about his neck and pitch him into one of the deepest holes of his dear Duddon.' He found Shelley 'too unsubstantial for me'. 'As for the modern Poetry', he admitted towards the end of his life, 'I have cared for none of the last thirty years, not even Tennyson, except in parts: pure, lofty, and noble as he always is. Much less can I endure the *Gurgoyle* school (I call it) begun, I suppose, by V. Hugo. . . .' He was sharply critical even of Tennyson, as he revealed in a letter to Donne:

> If one could have good Lyrics, I think the World wants them as much as ever. Tennyson's are good: but not of the kind wanted. . . . I felt that if Tennyson had got on a horse and ridden twenty miles, instead of moaning over his pipe, he would have been cured of his sorrows in half the time. As it is, it is about three years before the Poetic Soul walks itself out of darkness & Despair into Common Sense—Plato w^d not have allowed such querulousness to be published in his Republic, to be sure: and when we think of the Miss Barretts, Brownes, Jewsburys &c who will set to work to feel friends' losses in melodious tears, in imitation of A.T.'s—one must allow Plato was no such prig as some say he was.

FitzGerald's disapproval of modern poetry was not, however, so sweeping as he pretended: when in 1848 Richard Monckton Milnes published the *Life and Letters of John Keats*, FitzGerald was among the first to read them; and he was understandably swept off his feet: 'By the by', he ordered Tennyson's brother, 'beg, borrow, steal or buy Keats' Letters and Poems, written off-hand at a sitting most of them: I only wonder that they do not make a noise in the world.' Thirty years later we find him admonishing Fanny Kemble to read the Monckton Milnes *Life and Letters*, 'in which you will find what you may not have guessed from his Poetry (though almost unfathomably deep in that also) the strong, masculine, Sense and Humour, etc., of the man: more akin to Shakespeare, I am tempted to think, in a perfect circle of Poetic Faculties, than any Poet since'. Matthew Arnold and Middleton Murry were not alone in endorsing FitzGerald's judgement.

And whatever FitzGerald's strictures, he had a high regard for Tennyson: 'One must', he wrote, 'have labourers of different kinds in the vineyard of morality.... Wordsworth is first in the craft: but Tennyson does no little by raising and filling the brain with noble images and thoughts, which ... prepare and fit us for the reception of the higher philosophy.' He would gladly sit up till the small hours of the morning, heavy with influenza, while Tennyson recited 'some of his magic music'. But 'what astonishes me', he told Mrs. Cowell, 'is Shakespeare: when I look into him it is not a Book, but People talking all round me.... Milton seems a Dead-weight compared'. 'I have been reading Shakespeare's Sonnets,' he wrote to Allen, 'and I believe I am unprejudiced when I say that I had but half an idea of him, Demigod as he seemed before, till I read them carefully.... I have truly been lapped in these Sonnets for some time: they seem all stuck about my heart, like the ballads that used to be on the walls of London.'

* * *

Yet, when all is said, we do not read the letters of FitzGerald to discover his criticism of the arts; we read them, especially, because they reveal himself: serene, detached, unhurried, slightly wistful, with a humour, a modesty, a poetry of his own that touches the heart. And revelation is not, perhaps, the word to use of FitzGerald; for it has been truly said that 'there is a sense of kindly mystery about him, and we don't want to account for him. We are glad to have him as he is.' 'I think', wrote FitzGerald himself, 'I shall become rather a Bore, for I certainly do write Letters which I should not if I had proper occupation. . . .' His diffidence is part of his charm; to read FitzGerald's letters is, inescapably, to love him.

* * *

Of the quoting from FitzGerald there is no end. His sudden poetry, his Romantic melancholy, his touching modesty, his Elian, Keatsian humours: they make his letters constantly alive. True, he discusses the great men of his time; but such portraits remain unimportant beside the authentic picture of himself. FitzGerald is always a man of sensibility; he is rarely self-conscious, he is always sincere. He scribbles (it seems that he talks) on the spur of the moment: he writes, as he once described it, 'whatever-about-ly'. His thoughts 'go floating about in a gossamer way'. He is a man of taste and genius who likes 'to sail before the wind over the surface of an ever-rolling eloquence'. But his letters are not merely fine because they are admirable prose. They are masterly because they come from the heart.

It is difficult to place him in English literature. In time (and in certain features) he was eminently Victorian. He was a regular churchgoer; he was bewildered by religious controversy; he was acutely conscious of his duties towards his social inferiors; he urged educational reform; he was (though Irish) intensely patriotic. And yet, so often, as one reads his translations or his letters, one discerns the Romantic born out of his time: his *mal du siècle*, his pastoral and exotic interests, his morbidity, his humour and chivalry. FitzGerald was no Victorian philosopher: indeed 'it really gives me pain', he wrote, 'to hear you or anyone else call me a philosopher. . . . I am none, never was , . . . Some things, such as wealth, rank, respectability, I don't care a straw about . . .'. Such a comment struck at the roots of Victorian society.

FitzGerald, like all great men of letters, cannot be neatly classified. He belongs to, and stands apart from, his age. Browning, in a moment of fury, dismissed him as 'the wretched Irish fribble and feather-head'; Tennyson, in the birthday poem addressed to him, acclaimed 'Old Fitz' as a divine translator, and the *Rubáiyát* as a golden poem, 'a planet to the sun which cast it'. FitzGerald himself, with his usual diffidence, decided: 'I have not the strong inward call, nor cruel-sweet pangs of parturition, that proves the birth of anything bigger than a mouse. . . . I am a man of taste, of whom there are hundreds born every year.'

FitzGerald's judgement was quashed by his contemporaries; it will always be contradicted by posterity. His *Rubáiyát* is indeed a golden poem; his letters sometimes touch the epistolary heights. When he called himself a man of taste, he had perhaps forgotten his own aphorism: taste is the feminine of genius.

EDWARD FITZGERALD

A Select Bibliography

(*Place of publication London, unless stated otherwise*)

Bibliographies:

NOTES FOR A BIBLIOGRAPHY, by W. F. Prideaux (1901).
—there are also useful lists of the editions of the *Rubáiyát* and of articles about FitzGerald and Omar Khayyám in Glyde's *Life* (q.v.).

A BIBLIOGRAPHY OF THE RUBÁIYÁT OF OMAR KHAYYÁM, by A. G. Potter (1929).

BIBLIOGRAPHIES OF TWELVE VICTORIAN AUTHORS, by T. G. Ehrsam and R. H. Deily. New York (1936).
—supplement for FitzGerald by J. G. Fucilla in *Modern Philology*, xxxviii, 1939.

Collected Works:

WORKS, 2 vols. New York (1887).

LETTERS AND LITERARY REMAINS, edited by W. Aldis Wright. 3 vols. (1889).
—extended to 7 vols., incorporating the three following Collections of Letters, 1902–03.

LETTERS, edited by W. Aldis Wright. 2 vols. (1894).
—with 43 new letters.

LETTERS . . . TO FANNY KEMBLE, 1871–83, edited by W. Aldis Wright (1895).

MISCELLANIES, edited by W. Aldis Wright (1900).
—contains Omar Khayyám; Euphranor; Polonius; Salámán and Absál; Memoir of Bernard Barton; Death of Bernard Barton; Death of the Rev. George Crabbe.

MORE LETTERS, edited by W. Aldis Wright (1901).

THE VARIORUM AND DEFINITIVE EDITION OF THE POETICAL AND PROSE WRITINGS, edited by G. Bentham. 7 vols. New York (1902).
— does not include the correspondence.

SOME NEW LETTERS, edited by F. R. Barton (1923).

LETTERS . . . TO BERNARD QUARITCH 1853–83, edited by C. Q. Wrentmore (1926).

A FITZGERALD FRIENDSHIP, edited by C. B. Johnson and N. C. Hannay (1932).
—includes unpublished letters to W. B. Donne.

RUBÁIYÁT OF OMAR KHAYYÁM, RENDERED INTO ENGLISH VERSE BY EDWARD FITZGERALD. EUPHRANOR, A DIALOGUE ON YOUTH, SALÁMÁN AND ABSÁL, edited by G. F. Maine (1953).
—with an introduction by L. Housman.

Separate Works:

EUPHRANOR: A DIALOGUE ON YOUTH (1851). *Prose.*
—*Euphranor* went into three editions during FitzGerald's lifetime; edited by F. Chapman, 1906.

POLONIUS: A COLLECTION OF WISE SAWS AND MODERN INSTANCES (1852). *Prose.*
—new editions, 1903 and 1905.

SIX DRAMAS OF CALDERÓN, FREELY TRANSLATED (1853). *Drama.*
—in Everyman's Library [1928].

SALÁMÁN AND ABSÁL: AN ALLEGORY FREELY TRANSLATED FROM THE PERSIAN OF JÁMÍ (1856). *Verse.*
—third edition, 1879, with the fourth edition of the *Rubáiyát*. Comparative edition, edited by A. J. Arberry, 1956, with an introduction based on unpublished letters between FitzGerald and Edward Cowell.

RUBÁIYÁT OF OMAR KHAYYÁM, THE ASTRONOMER POET OF PERSIA (1859). *Verse.*
—revised translation, 1868, 1872, 1879. Variorum edition in two volumes, edited by N. H. Dole, 1898, with English, French, German, Italian and Danish translations, and bibliographies. Concordance, edited by J. R. Tutin, 1900.

THE MIGHTY MAGICIAN and SUCH STUFF AS DREAMS ARE MADE ON (1865). *Drama.*
—two plays translated from Calderón. Incorporated, with the six previously published, in *Eight Dramas of Calderón*, 1906.

THE TWO GENERALS. I. Lucius Aemitius Paullus. II. Sir Charles Napier. *Verse.*
—two poems, privately printed, *c.* 1865.

AGAMEMNON, A TRAGEDY TAKEN FROM AESCHYLUS [1876]. *Drama.*
—privately printed.

THE DOWNFALL AND DEATH OF KING OEDIPUS (Part I, 1880; Part II, 1881).
Drama.
—privately printed.

READINGS IN CRABBE'S 'TALES OF THE HALL' (1882). *Prose.*
—originally privately printed [1879].

OCCASIONAL VERSES (1891).
—privately printed.

DICTIONARY OF MADAME DE SÉVIGNÉ, edited by M. E. FitzGerald Kerrich.
2 vols. (1914). *Prose.*

Some Critical and Biographical Studies:

TWO SUFFOLK FRIENDS, by F. H. Groome (1895).
—a reprint of two intimate articles from *Blackwood's Magazine* on FitzGerald and R. C. Groome, the author's father.

SOME SIDELIGHTS UPON EDWARD FITZGERALD'S POEM 'THE RUBÁIYÁT OF OMAR KHAYYÁM', by E. Heron-Allen (1898).
—a reprinted lecture, designed to show that FitzGerald's *Rubáiyát* was not only a remarkable paraphrase, but 'a synthetical result of our poet's entire course of Persian studies'.

EDWARD FITZGERALD AND OMAR KHAYYÁM: AN ESSAY AND BIBLIOGRAPHY (1899).

THE LIFE, by J. Glyde (1900).
—with an Introduction by E. Clodd. A moralising but worthy book, with useful bibliographies.

EDWARD AND PAMELA FITZGERALD, BEING SOME ACCOUNT OF THEIR LIVES COMPILED FROM LETTERS OF THOSE WHO KNEW THEM, by G. Campbell (1904).

THE LIFE, by T. Wright. 2 vols. (1904).
—a solid and competent account.

EDWARD FITZGERALD, by A. C. Benson (1905).
—in the English Men of Letters series. Benson drew chiefly on Wright's *Life* for his bibliographical data.

EDWARD FITZGERALD AND 'POSH': 'HERRING MERCHANTS', by J. Blyth (1908).
—including a number of letters from Edward FitzGerald to Joseph Fletcher or 'Posh', not hitherto published.

OMAR'S INTERPRETER. A NEW LIFE OF EDWARD FITZGERALD, by M. Adams (1909).
—revised edition, 1911.

IN THE FOOTSTEPS OF BORROW AND FITZGERALD, by M. Adams (1913).
ÉTUDE SUR EDWARD FITZGERALD ET LA LITTÉRATURE PERSANE, D'APRÈS LES SOURCES ORIGINALES, par J-M. H. Thonet. Liége (1929).

THE LIFE OF EDWARD FITZGERALD, TRANSLATOR OF THE RUBÁIYÁT OF OMAR KHAYYÁM, by A. M. Terhune. New Haven (1947).
—the most up-to-date and comprehensive study. It contains a good deal of new material, but it is dully written.

INTO AN OLD ROOM: A MEMOIR OF FITZGERALD, by P. de Polnay. New York (1949).
—by a novelist who lived in Fitzgerald's Suffolk home for some years.

OMAR KHAYYÁM, by A. J. Arberry. New Haven (1952).